Lyrics from Cotton Land

BY

JOHN CHARLES McNEILL

Drawings by A. B. Frost and E. W. Kemble

CHARLOTTE, N. C.
STONE PUBLISHING CO.

SOLE DISTRIBUTORS:
SAM'L GABRIEL SONS & CO.
NEW YORK

Copyright, 1922, By
CHARLES S. STONE

Copyright, 1949, By
THE UNIVERSITY OF NORTH CAROLINA PRESS

PUBLISHER'S NOTE

MANY of these verses have been published in the *Charlotte Observer,* some in the *Century Magazine,* and the others appear first in this book. To the *Observer* and the *Century* are due thanks for their permission to republish.

INTRODUCTION.

THE story of a rare, gifted soul is difficult to write. The commonplace man is usually the resultant of forces that can be calculated. The measuring line can be laid to his life; dates, places and movements assume great significance. But it is not so with the man who approaches genius. His soul is a mystery; its birth and growth defy explanation; dates and circumstances mean little. To write a true biography of such a man, incidents and experiences must be known that lie beyond the research of the scientific student. Such a man was the author of the poems contained in this volume. And, although custom compels to write the usual facts of birth and movement, they are written briefly, in the knowledge that they have little significance for the life of the gifted spirit which sang these songs to men.

John Charles McNeill was the second son of Duncan and Euphemia Livingston McNeill, and was born at their country place, near Laurinburg, in Richmond county, N. C., on July 26, 1874.

INTRODUCTION

He grew to manhood on his father's farm, living the free, happy, normal life of the country boy. On the surface these early years seem to have been uneventful; they were marked by no unusual experiences or incidents. Work, study, and play seem to tell the story. But the achievements of his maturer years show these early days to have been the determining, formative period of his life. A careful and sympathetic examination of his writings discovers the fact that almost all the dreams, visions, loves, adorations and ecstasies to which he gave such beautiful expression, came to him in the honest work, clean, healthful play and idle roaming about wood and field, in those early and, always to him, happy days. He knew and loved all the sights, voices and moods of nature; he was nature's child, and was true through all after years to this Mother of the Mystery.

In 1893 McNeill entered Wake Forest College. The college records show that he was an unusual student, and in English his work was little less than brilliant. He was tutor in this department in his first year, won the Dixon medal, given to the best essayist of each year, and was editor-in-chief of the "Wake Forest Student." He graduated valedictorian of his class in 1898. The period immediately following his graduation seems

INTRODUCTION

to have been one of uncertainty and unhappiness to him. He returned to Wake Forest to take his master's degree, worked as instructor in English, and studied law. During the year 1899-1900, he filled the Chair of English in Mercer University, at Macon, Georgia, in the absence of the professor of English, and did admirable work. In 1900 he returned to North Carolina and began the practice of law at Lumberton. He often said to the writer that he was happy in none of these things. He was evidently striving to find himself.

McNeill had some success in the practice of his profession, and he was elected to represent the people of his county in the State Legislature. But his heart was in other things. He would often shut his office door to friend and client and try to write out some vision that floated in his soul. The "Century Magazine" accepted and published some of his productions and asked for other contributions. He did work for a local paper and wrote occasionally for various papers and journals. More and more he came to find his joy in self-expression; and his writing began to attract the attention of the public.

In 1904 the "Charlotte Observer" discovered the promise in this gifted man, and gave him his chance. He was attached to the staff of that

INTRODUCTION

paper and given perfect liberty of action. He could write what he pleased and when he pleased, and received for his work a regular and adequate compensation. Under such treatment he found himself. His soul seemed to burst into blossom; and during the three years of his connection with the "Observer" he gave to the world almost all his best work. In 1905 he was awarded the Patterson Cup, and a year later published his first volume of poems under the title "Songs, Merry and Sad." Although this volume was published by a local firm, it found ready sale and the edition was soon exhausted.

In the early months of 1907 some disease, baffling to friends and physicians alike, began to take hold upon him. For months he fought a brave fight against it and seemed for a while to be regaining his strength. But, suddenly, almost without warning, acute nephritis attacked him and he fell its victim, dying on the 17th of October, 1907.

McNeill was a man of unusual physical appearance; his tall, straight, slender figure, his thick iron-gray hair and handsome features made him a marked man in any company. His eyes were remarkable. In his careless moods there was nothing unusual in them; but when his soul was aflame with some inner vision, his eyes glowed

INTRODUCTION

with a light that was both beautiful and compelling in its magnetism.

He had the open, free and cordial manner of the gentleman born and reared in the country. He knew little and cared less for social conventions. There was about him that charming unconsciousness of self that one so often sees in the people who live close to and love the genuine things of nature. It is the estimate of all who knew him well that McNeill was one of the most lovable of men. His unselfishness, his freedom from cant and pretension, his love of and joy in life, his perfect candor and his power to love and be interested in the people about him, made him a peerless friend. And in many the sorrow for the loss to the State and Nation of this fine, rare and gifted spirit, was overshadowed by a sense of personal bereavement.

THE PATTERSON MEMORIAL CUP.

Magnificent Trophy as an Incentive to the Development of Literary Talent in North Carolina.

Philadelphia, March 24.—As a memorial to her father, the late Colonel William Houston Patterson, of this city, and as an incentive to the development of the literary talent of the sons and daughters of the Old North State, Mrs. Lindsay Patterson, of Winston-Salem, has had manufactured here one of the most massive and magnificent loving cups that Philadelphia jewelers have ever seen. This cup is to be presented to the North Carolina Historical Society, and by that society is at the end of the year to be turned over to that resident, native North Carolina writer who shall have achieved the greatest literary success during the year. At the end of ten years, it is to become the property of the person who shall have won it the greatest number of times.

Because of its extraordinary beauty, and because of the story of filial love behind it, it has attracted great attention.

THE PATTERSON MEMORIAL CUP

The cup is of gold and of massive construction. It stands 16 inches high, and is seven inches in diameter. On the bases of the three handles are the coats of arms of North Carolina, Pennsylvania and the Patterson family. It is studded with forty-nine precious stones, all being North Carolina gems, selected by Mrs. Patterson from over 400 specimens. It bears the inscriptions: "The William Houston Patterson Cup," and "Cor Cordium" (Heart of Hearts). — Philadelphia Correspondent to "Charlotte (N. C.) Observer."

PRESENTATION OF PATTERSON MEMORIAL CUP.

In the Senate Chamber in the State Capitol, Thursday morning, October 19, 1905, President Theodore Roosevelt, representing the North Carolina Literary and Historical Association, presented to Mr. John Charles McNeill, of Charlotte, the Patterson Memorial Cup, awarded him for having published during the preceding twelve months work showing "the greatest excellence and the highest literary skill and genius." Lieutenant-Governor Winston, representing the Governor, presented the newly-elected President of the Association, ex-Governor C. B. Aycock, who then stated the object of the Cup and the conditions of the award. According to the notes furnished by Mr. Loeb, the President said:

"MR. MCNEILL: I feel, and I am sure all good Americans must feel, that it is far from enough for us to develop merely a great material prosperity. I appreciate, and all of us must, that it is indispensable to have the material prosperity as

PRESENTATION OF PATTERSON MEMORIAL CUP

a foundation, but if we think the foundation is the entire building, we never shall rank as among the nations of the world; and therefore it is with peculiar pleasure that I find myself playing a small part in a movement, such as this, by which one of the thirteen original States, one of our great States, marks its sense of proper proportion in estimating the achievements of life, the achievements of which the Commonwealth has a right to be proud. It is a good thing to have the sense of historic continuity with the past, which we get largely through the efforts of just such historic societies as this, through which this Cup is awarded to you. It is an even better thing to try to do what we can to show our pleasure in and approval of productive literary work in the present. Mr. McNeill, I congratulate you and North Carolina."

Mr. McNeill's reply follows:

"Mr. President, my joy in this golden trophy is heightened by the fortune which permits me to take it from the hand of the foremost citizen of the world. To you, sir, to Mrs. Lindsay Patterson, our gracious matron of letters, and to the committee of scholars whose judgment was kind to me, all thanks."

CONTENTS

	PAGE
Mr. Nigger	1
Spring	4
Hardihood	6
A Protest	7
Preacherly Preference	8
Springtime	9
One Sided	11
'T Ain't Long	13
Bluffers	14
Nigger Demus	15
Wishing	18
The Catfish	20
Folk Song	23
Three Hypotheses	24
A Modest Ploughman	26
The August Meeting	29
Salutations	32
Po' Baby	33
'Ligion	34
A Few Days Off	35
Noontime	37

CONTENTS

	PAGE
DISEASES	39
A TAR HEEL	41
EVERY MAN'S WAY	42
A SUMMER RESORT	43
THE TRICKSTER TRICKED	45
BE SHAME	50
A DREAM OF YOU	51
ENVIRONMENT	53
'POSSUM TIME AGAIN	55
NOAH'S ARK	56
A MONOLOGUE	62
DE THREE FROSTIES	63
PUNISHMENT	64
OBEDIENCE	65
WEATHER SIGNALS	66
UTOPIA	67
THE RACCOON	68
THE CROW'S SHADOW	70
IN A CANOE	72
NAMING THE ANIMALS	75
THE RED SHIRTS	77
POOR OLD BEN	79
FOR CORN SHUCKINGS	81
ONE DAY	82
A HINDRANCE	84
A PALLET SLEEPER	86
SUBSTITUTES	87

CONTENTS

	PAGE
BEDTIME	89
THE PERSIMMON TREE	91
"BELIEVING WHERE WE CANNOT PROVE"	94
CONVENIENT THEOLOGY	95
BABY'S NOGGIN	97
BLACK MOLASSES	98
OLD AUNT PLEASANT	100
THE CROWN OF POWER	103
THE REJECTED SCOTSMAN	104
A SOFT SNAP	109
AMBITION	110
THE SIESTA	112
THE DIEDIPER	114
SNAKES	116
MYSTERIES	118
BABY'S LEGS	119
GRASS	120
THE VARMINT CONVENTION	121
THE COON FROM THE COLLEGE TOWN	124
IF	126
TOT AND TED	127
BOYS' VISIONS	130
HOLDING OFF THE CALF	133
WHEN THE CALVES GET OUT	135
CATS	137
TO ALFONSO XIV	141
A TOMTIT MESSENGER	144

CONTENTS

	PAGE
TO ONE WHO IS GOOD	146
DEW	147
RACE SUICIDE	148
THE FIRST FLOWER	150
DEAD	152
VIEWPOINTS	155
OLD JIM SWINK	156
THE DOODLE BUG	159
AUTUMN	163
THE THREE TOTS	165
AT THE DANCE	167
SELFISHNESS	171
DESERTED	173
GRANDADDY-LONG-LEGS	174
THE CASTLE BUILDER	175
TO-MORROW	177
A CHOICE	179
THE IRON DOOR	181
THE TENANT	183
HORSEMINT	184
IN THE WOODS	186
TO SLEEP	188

MR. NIGGER

How could we do without you,
      Mr. Nigger?
Could we not talk about you,
      Mr. Nigger,
We 'd have to quit our politics,
'T would put our papers in a fix,
We 'd have to start and learn new tricks,
      Mr. Nigger.

Ah, ragtime would be sadly misst,
      Mr. Nigger!
There 'd be no elocutionist,
      Mr. Nigger.
The coon-song's flow would then be checked,
The minstrel show would soon be wrecked
And writers of your dialect,
      Mr. Nigger.

LYRICS FROM COTTON LAND

I cannot see, if you were dead,
      Mr. Nigger,
How orators could earn their bread,
      Mr. Nigger;
For they could never hold the crowd
Save they abused you long and loud
As being a dark and threatening cloud,
      Mr. Nigger.

But plough my land and barn my crop,
      Mr. Nigger.
I'll furnish sorghum for your sop,
      Mr. Nigger.
And see you earn your money's worth,
Else, when dull times possess the earth,
I'll burn you to excite the North,
      Mr. Nigger.

You're a vast problem to our hand,
      Mr. Nigger.

MR. NIGGER

Your fame is gone throughout the land,
    Mr. Nigger.
The heart of all this mighty nation
Is set to work out your salvation,
But don't you fear expatriation,
    Mr. Nigger.

SPRING

I AXED de chillun fer de joke
   Dat made 'em laugh en run.
"It ain't no joke," dey says; "we 's jis'
   Er-natchly havin' fun."

I axed a rooster mockin'bird,
   When I had cotch his eye,
"Why does you sing all day en night?"
   Says he, "I dunno why."

I axed a yearlin' why he pawed
   De dust up in de lane.
He bellered out his sass, "Boo-boo!
   I feels lak raisin' cain!"

SPRING

En den de chillun, bird, en kef
  Axed why I felt so good.
S' I, "Don't ax me. Kerwhoop!" says I.
  "It 's supp'n' in my blood!"

HARDIHOOD

De drouf hit pahched our crap at fust
    En de rain done drown it now,
But whe'r it freshet or whe'r it dust
    De crabgrass gwine a grow,
        Grow,
    De crabgrass gwine a grow.

De cawn jis' want some scuse to quit,
    En cotton's a reg'lar chile,
But de sun kin scawch en de rain kin spit,
    But de crabgrass wear a smile,
        Smile,
    De crabgrass wear a smile.

A PROTEST

De cawn is drapped en civered
  Fer de crow to grabble out.
De shoat he fin's de 'tater bed
  Befo' dey 'gins to sprout.

De hen hatch out her chickens
  Whilst de hawk bees lookin' on,
En 'fo' de cherries ripens good
  De birds is got 'em gone.

Dey all steals fum de nigger man,
  But if de nigger steals
Dey putts him on de chaingang
  Wid a weight behin' his heels.

PREACHERLY PREFERENCE

I LAKS to plough in a stubble fiel'
  Among de dews en damps,
Whar now en den yo' plough turns up
  A passle er fox-fire lamps.
De dirt slide off er de turn-plough whing
  En rumple in turnin' over,
Wid de dead crab-grass en de dead peavines
  En a few green clumps er clover.

But keep me out er de new-groun' lan',
  'Ca'se I 's a preacher, boss,
En no preacher wa'n't made fer no new-groun' han'
  Behin' no fidgity hoss.
De roots, en switches, en stumps, en hol's,
  En de briers—I tells you plain,
When I ploughs sich new-groun' lan', it gives
  My 'ligion a powerful strain!

SPRINGTIME

O CATFISH in de eddy,
   When de moon is in de full!
O watermillion ready
   'Mongs' yo' dewy leaves, to pull!
O choofies, sugar-rooted!
   Us women en us men
Is all done back bar'footed,
   'Ca'se de springtime's come again.

De bullbat 'gins to beller
   Across de shimmery hill.
'T ain't long befo' a feller
   Kin hear de whuppoorwill.
De hawk sets roun' en watches
   De biddies wid de hen,
Er-scratchin' in de doodle dust,
   'Ca'se springtime's come again.

LYRICS FROM COTTON LAND

Dirt-daubers soon be squealin',
   Shapin' up deir mud,
En a sort er sleepy feelin'
   'Ll git gwine along yo' blood,
Till you lose yo' holt, en dozes,
   En jerks, en wakes up—den
De fus' thing dat you knows is
   Dat de springtime's come again.

ONE SIDED

Is I boun' to keep de Sabbath day,
   When de hawk goes free?
Is I boun' to set in my yahd en pray
En let dem crows in de cawn-patch stay
En grabble en tote my cawn away?
   Hit's funny to me!

If de varmints 'll knock-off workin', too,
   En set in de sun,
I'll rest en pray de whole day thoo;
But, if dey goes loose en is gwine a do
Wut dey pleases, den 'tain't Shoo, shoo!
   But it's Bang! wid de gun.

It's mighty po' rest to be shet in a stall,
   Lak you got no sense;

It's mighty po' prayin' when de watch-crow call
Fum de scare-crow's head, en de chicken squall;
En it's mighty po' 'ligion when Sunday's all
  Dis side er de fence!

'T AIN'T LONG

TIE a new cracker
  Upon de ol' lash;
Roll up de log heaps
  En burn all de trash;
Scooter de newgroun',
  Dreen out de pon';
Bone off fer cotton
  En bed up fer cawn.

'T ain't long 'fo' drappin'
  De seed in de groun';
'T ain't long 'fo' choppin'
  En sidin' aroun';
'T ain't long 'fo' tassels
  En blooms gits in prime;
Uh-uh! it ain't long
  'Fo' layin'-by time!

BLUFFERS

Buzzin' white-nose bumblebee,
   Buzz en buzz yo' whing;
Dart off faster 'n I kin see,
En shoot back whar you used to be.
You can't putt no bluff on me:
   You don't tote no sting!

Adder, hissin' at my toe,
   You ain't got no p'ison!
Draw yo' head en strack yo' blow.
Spread yo' jaws wide out, jis' so.
You can't fool me. You don't know
   Who you got yo' eyes on.

NIGGER DEMUS

Dis is anudder Sunday when I done fugit my
    specks.
I 'll hatter 'pen', my bruddern, 'pon de 'memb'-
    ance er de tex'.
'N' if you-all wants a snow-white tent up hyander
    in de skies
You better keep de Scripters in yo' head, en not
    yo' eyes.

Now, while de hat is pas' aroun' by Bill en Poly-
    phemus,
I 's gwine a tell you supp'n' 'bout dat gre't man,
    Nigger Demus—
But watch de hat, my bruddern, when dey goes
    to make deir change:
Dey's good folks, but in spite er dat don't give
    'em too much range.

LYRICS FROM COTTON LAND

Ol' Nigger Demus come by night, as we is 'sembled now;
He didn' have time to come by day, beca'se he had to plough;
En Jawn de Baptis' met him en he ax him whar he 's gwine,
En Demus say he want to know wut chu'ch he better jine.

Jawn watch' a cloud across de moon, en study little while.
En den he turnt to Demus en he says, "You makes me smile."
Says 'e, "De Baptis' chu'ch," he says, " 's de chu'ch you otter jine,
'Ca'se, glory halleloolyer! in de fus' place, it is mine.

"En den," says 'e, "it 's natchel: de dog he lacks to swim,
But it take' a sight er creepin' 'fo' you git to sprinkle him;

NIGGER DEMUS

De tarpin he look up en see a shower comin' on,
En chook! he dive' fum off his log deep down into de pon'."

"Dat 's so," says Demus—dat a-way—"I laks to dive myse'f,
But 'fo' de rain kin ketch me, Jawn, I sho runs out er bref.
So some day when it 's good en warm en de sun come out to shine,
You tell me whar yo' chu'ch is at, beca'se I 'ten's to jine."

He didn' know no doctrine, but he knowed a sign en wonder,
En so he went wid Jawn one day, en Jawn he putt him under.
En dat's why Sal en Bill en Ben en Heck en ol' Br'er Remus
En all de niggers jine de chu'ch jis' same as Nigger Demus.

WISHING

I wisht I wus a hummin' bird.
   I 'd nes' in a willer tree.
Den noth'n' but supp'n' wut goes on wings
   Could ever git to me.

I wisht I wus a snake. I 'd crawl
   Down in a deep stump hole.
Noth'n' 'u'd venture down in dar,
   Into de dark en col'.

But jis' a nigger in his shack,
   Wid de farlight in de chinks—
Supp'n' kin see him ever' time
   He even so much as winks.

WISHING

It 's a natchel fac' dat many a time
   I wisht I wus supp'n' wil';
A coon or a' owl or a possum or crow—
   Leas'ways, a little while.

I 'd lak to sleep in a holler gum
   Or roost in a long-leaf pine,
Whar nothin' 'u'd come to mess wid me
   Or ax me whar I 's gwine.

THE CATFISH

When de nights is warm en de moon is full,
You kin ketch mo' cats dan you cares to pull.
   No trouble 'bout de bait;
A grub 'll do or a li'l' fat meat,
Fer all he wants is supp'n' to eat,
   En he ain't no han' to wait.

Ner dar ain't no trouble 'bout luck wid him.
You kin tie yo' line to a swingin' limb,
   En when you goes to look,
You'll fin' dat limb a-dodgin' roun',
En bubbles risin' en floatin' on down,
   En a catfish on yo' hook.

But I chooses to take a pole in mine
En git in a splotch er bright moonshine

THE CATFISH

"I LETS HIM SHOW HIS MAN"

LYRICS FROM COTTON LAND

En fish dar wid my han';
I knows, den, when he hits his lick
(He swallows de hook; you needn' be quick),
En I lets him show his man.

When I slings him out on de good dry grass,
He don't complain, but he's full er sass.
He kicks a little while,
Den lays dar, wid a pleasing look,
En, while I's rippin' out de hook,
He takes it wid a smile.

FOLK SONG

If you don't b'lieve dat train kin run,
      Honey;
If you don't b'lieve dat train kin run,
Come en lemme tell you wut de train done done,
      Honey.

It lef' Savanner at de settin' er de sun,
      Honey;
It lef' Savanner at de settin' er de sun,
En it fotch me home by half-pas' one,
      Honey!

THREE HYPOTHESES

If Marse Adam wus white, Rose Anner,
   If Miss Eve wus white lak him
(Dat's how de pictures makes 'em;
   De Scriptur' 's a leetle dim),
Den whar did de nigger come fum?
   'T wus a pine wid a 'simmon limb;
If Marse Adam wus white, Rose Anner,
   En Miss Eve wus white lak him.

If Nora wus white, my honey
   (Nora wut built de ark)
Den de nigger 's a sort er a bluebird
   Hatch out fum de egg er a lark.
But dat don't never happen,
   En dat question still bees dark,
If Nora wus white, my honey,
   En his chillun in dat ark.

THREE HYPOTHESES

I is a sunburnt white man,
   'F a minner 's a little trout.
You mus' go deeper'n dis here hide
   To git de nigger out.
'F you skint me slam fum head to heel,
   New nigger-hide 'u'd sprout.
Yas; I's a sunburnt white man—
   'F a minner's a little trout.

A MODEST PLOUGHMAN

When crabgrass gits a half a show,
'Count er some rainy days, to grow
En fuzzes green along de row,
'T ain't wuth while den to try to hoe
  Dat whole plantation clean.
De bes' way is de way dat 's cheap,
En I kin take a two-inch sweep,
Runnin' at p'int two inches deep,
  En kill out Gineral Green.

Yes; gimme sich a plow as dat
'N' I 'll hol' my upright frame plum flat,
En whar dat grass wus sich a mat

A MODEST PLOUGHMAN

You couldn' tell whar a hoe been at,
   I 'll wrop dat cotton roun'
As neat en cool wid fresh black dirt
As a man's body fits his shirt,
En reg'lar—not right here a spurt
   En hyander grassy groun'.

Farmers is got a heap to l'arn
'Fo' dey gits wut 's comin' to deir barn.
If, 'stid er har'n' hoe-han's en har'n'
Plough-han's wut ain't wuth a darn,
   Dey 'd all git men lak me,
Dis county 'd brag de bigges' sales
Er cotton seed en cotton bales,
Spite er spring drouth en 'noctial gales,
   On dis side er de sea.

En dis ain't whoopin' up myse'f.
De crabgrass natchly hol' its bref
When I comes 'long; 'ca'se dat means de'f;
It knows dar ain't none gwine be lef',

Whar I has made my tracks.
I says dis jis' beca'se it 's so.
I kinder thought you 'd lak to know.
Don't think I 's tryin' to brag en blow;
   I allus deals in fac's.

THE AUGUST MEETING

    It wus at our Augus' meetin'
    When dar wa'n't nigh room fer seatin'
All de sinners en de saved wut come to it;
    But dar wa'n't no pride en poutin';
    Dey fell in line to shoutin'
Lak dey 's gwine git all de 'ligion dey could git.

    I ain't er-tryin' to fool you,
    But when Heck bawl, "Halleloolyer!"
All dem niggers bounce right up en 'gin to prance.
    En when ol' Heck would holler
    Den dem common coons would foller,
Till de flo' wus full er people in a trance.

    You could see de preacher swayin'
    En er-preachin' en er-prayin',

But you couldn' hear de loudes' word he sayed.
  De benches kep' er-breakin',
  En de fuss dey kep' er-makin'
'Peared wuss 'n all de fuss dey 'd done en made.

  Now, Ander is a nigger
  Wut 's too quick upon de trigger;
His eyes is white as snow, his gums is blue;
  When Heck ram' up ag'in' 'im,
  De scrappin' blood riz in 'im,
En he retch en fotch his razor fum his shoe.

  Some ubbm friz to Ander,
  En dey hilt Heck over hyander,
Whilst de chillun en de gals wus runnin' out.
  Den Heck haul back en hit 'im,
  Dat bluegum nigger bit 'im,
En de whole chu'ch full er gemmen up en fou't.

  Dar wus razors, knives, en wrenches;
  Planks fum offen busted benches,
En some ubbm made a club er deir brogans.

THE AUGUST MEETING

  Oh, dey putt one ner to sleepin'
  Wid ever' sort er weepin',
En I seed one fool er-fightin' wid his han's.

  Wid all deir fights en trances,
  Deir holy shakes en dances,
Dey stayed dar till de roosters 'gun to crow;
  En de rain beat out de cotton,
  De fodder hung dar, rotten,
En de shattered peas wus sproutin' in de row.

SALUTATIONS

How is you dis mornin'?
  I 's so 's to be about.
En yo' ol' man is well, I hopes?
  Yes; he gits in en out.
En how is all de fambly?
  Dey ain't complainin' none.
En yo' po' conju'd, hoodooed boy?
  Lak a lizzud in de sun.

PO' BABY

Wut make' you keep on cryin' en cryin'?
  I do' know wut to do.
Dar ain't no pin dat I kin fin'
  Er-stickin' in you.

I b'lieve you 's jis' er-makin' out,
  Er-thinkin' maybe
Dat I 's er-gwine a tote you 'bout,
  Sayin', "Po', po' baby!"

Po' baby, is he feelin' sick?
  Po' baby, is he ailin'?
Come on! Less us play a trick!
  Whoopee! Ain't we sailin'!

'LIGION

De Augus' meetin' 's over now.
  We 's all done been baptize',
Me en Ham en Hick'ry Jim
  En Joe's big Lize.

Oh, 'ligion is a cu'i's thing
  In its workin' amongs' men!
We 'll hatter wait a whole yur now
  'Fo' bein' baptize' again!

A FEW DAYS OFF

I ain't gwine a work till my dyin' day;
   'F I ever lays up enough,
I's gwine a go off a while en stay;
   I'll be takin' a few days off.
'Ca'se de jimson weeds don't bloom but once,
   En when dey's shed dey's shed;
En when you 's dead, 'tain't jis' a few mont's,
   But you's gwine be a long time dead.

I knowed a' ol' man died powerful rich—
   Two mules en lan' en a cow.
I jis' soon die fum fallin' in a ditch,
   Fer he went to 's grave fum 's plow.
He never had nothin' 't wus good to eat
   Ner no piller upon his bed;
He never took time to dance wid his feet,
   But he's gwine a take a long time dead.

I knowed a' ol' ooman wut scrubbed en hoed,
    En never didn' go nowhar,
En when she died de people knowed
    Dat she had supp'n' hid 'bout dar.
She mought 'a' dressed up en 'a' done supp'n' wrong
    En had 'er a coht-case ple'd'.
But she didn' have time to live veh long;
    She's gwine have a plenty dead.

So I says, if I manage to save enough
    Fum de wages I gits dis yur,
I is right den takin' a few days off
    At one thing en an'er.
'Ca'se while I is got my mouf en eyes
    En a little wheel in my head,
I's gwine a live fas', fer when I dies
    I'll sho be a long time dead.

NOONTIME

My shadder shortened slow,
  Roun' by roun',
En I thought dat dinner horn
  'Ll'd never soun';
But de sun kep' on er-crawlin'
Till at las' dat horn wus callin',
En my lines wa'n't no time fallin'
  To de groun'.

When I laid dem harness back
  On de beam,
Dat mule he woke up wide
  En quit his dream.
He didn't need no paddle
En I didn't need no saddle.
Me en him—Skeedump, skeedaddle!—
  Wus a team!

If you 'd er-seed us gwine
  Home dat day,
You 'd 'a' thought 'twus dat wus gittin
  Us our pay,
Fer dat po' ol' sleepy critter
Made de geese en chickens scatter,
En her ol' feet went clap-clatter
  'Pon de clay.

Her feelin's wa'n't so powerful
  Fur fum mine.
It makes a differ'nce wut 's ahead
  En wut 's behin'.
Wh'er it 's to er fum de table,
Wh'er it 's in er out de stable,
Wut make you ail'n' er able
  'S whar you 's gwine.

DISEASES

(ILLUSTRATING FOLK ETYMOLOGY)

I once et too much sparrowgrass:
Dey thought I 's dead, 'll I breaved on glass.

Cornsumption wrastle mighty strong;
St. Fighter's dance fou't fast en long;

De foxfire got amongs' my spleen,
En yaller johnnies turnt me green;

Brownskeeters would n' lemme breave,
En de collard-marbles made me heave.

But I kyored myse'f, as you kin see,
Wid calamis root en horehoun' tea,

Ner all my life I ain't seed fit
To go to no horse-spittle yit.

But now, fer all de fights I 's fou't,
I 's feared at las' I 'll git knocked out,

Fer de toughest rail er all de riders
Is boun' to be dis pender-ciders.

When it hits a man, de only plan
Is to go right natchly in dat man,

En rummage 'roun' en kyarve about
Till you gits dat pender-ciders out.

No kine er calamis en tea
Gwine keep dat zease fum sett'n' you free,

En dis here nigger he don't brag,
But 'roun' his neck he totes a bag,

En in dat bag—jis' sniff en see—
Bees a ball er assyfidity!

A TAR HEEL

Oh, I gits my stren'th fum white-side meat,
I sops all de sorghum a nigger kin eat,
I chaws wheat bread on Saddy night,
En Sunday 's when my jug gits light.

I kin cut mo' boxes 'n a shorter while,
Den any 'er coon fer forty mile';
I kin dip mo' tar en scrape mo' scrape
En leave my crap in better shape,

En chip en pull en corner finer,
Den any 'er coon in No'th Killiner.
When it comes to bein' a turk'ntime han',
Count Loftin fer a full-size' man.

EVERY MAN'S WAY

Out in the town I 'd die if people knew
    I took this little glove and kissed it so;
Last thing at night, when footfall sounds are few
    And she who wore it sleeps as still as snow.

For, if they saw me, they would laugh, and I
    Should blush and drop my eyes and turn in shame
And curse me for a fondling fool and try
    To laugh and rob my folly of its fame.

But now the door is shut! and I can bless
    And kiss this wrinkled scrap, and care no whit
How great my heart may grow with tenderness
    Or what dear love-words I may say to it.

A SUMMER RESORT

Under and in a dogwood tree
   They 've made a modern fine hotel,
Owned by nobody but these three,
   Mary, Alex, and Isabel.

They 've laid the ground floor off in squares
   For rooms and hallways big enough;
The dogwood limbs are winding stairs
   Up to the leaves, which are the roof.

Down near the ground the tree sends out
   A fork, and thus it makes the door,
Where Alex stands or struts about,
   Both porter and proprietor.

Mary is cook and waitress too,
   Isabel she keeps the house,
And all three take their turns to do
   The milking of the Maypop cows.

This is to be a summer home
   For folks elsewhile in city pent,
And I, their press man, beg you come.
   (The weekly rate is flat one cent.)

Fear not lest you be turned outdoors.
   The place stands good for any boost.
For, if no ground space should be yours,
   They 'll put you on the stairs to roost.

THE TRICKSTER TRICKED

Long ways fum home I wus huntin' my cow.
   She'd done en los' her bell,
En which-a way she wus travelin', how
   Does you reckin I could tell?
Hongry en hot, weak en tar'd,
   I wus 'bout to turn aroun',
When I seed ol' Rattler grabblin' hard
   Atter supp'n' in de groun'.

I breaks a switch en twis' it 'bout
   Down dar, en den I pull
Till my holt break, en dat switch bring out
   A passle er 'possum wool!
'T wa'n't many minutes, bless yo' life,
   'Fo' I felt lak anudder man:
I wus gwine on home to see my wife
   Wid a 'possum in my han'!

Knowin' his ways, I hilt him so
   He couldn' ketch my pants.
He'd not take long to do his do
   'F I gin him half a chance.
'Twus up hill den, en down hill now,
   Lak a man wut's bein' paid—
When all er sudden I seed my cow
   Asleep in a dog'ood shade!

"Whoo-hee!" I hollered: up she flounce
   En her runnin' wus enough.
Right den I, too, wus on de bounce
   To head dat heifer off.
Fergittin' wut wus in my han',
   I flop him 'g'inst my shin.
It didn' take long to change my plan
   When I felt dem teef sink in.

At fust I tried to snatch him loose,
   But one jerk made me quit;
Dat varmint had to have some scuse

THE TRICKSTER TRICKED

"AT FUST I TRIED TO SNATCH HIM LOOSE"

Befo' he gwine a spit.
I laid down, lak I 'us fallin' sleep,
    Workin' de 'possum trick,
But smiles wus powerful hard to keep,
    'Ca'se it hurt lak a thousan' brick!

When he felt his tail done been sot free,
    He thought 'twus time to go.
I reck'n he jedged he 'us foolin' me,
    'Ca'se he open' his mouf right slow.
He started off—but we wa'n't gone fur
    'Fo' Rattler counted in,
En 'doubt no cradle or nairy a song,
    Putt him to sleep ag'in.

I let dat cow go on her way,
    Runnin' herse'f a race.
You kin drive yo' cow home any day,
    But a 'possum's meat is sca'ce.
Oh, I sucked his bones en sopped his juice.
    Thinks I, "Now wa'n't dat slick!

THE TRICKSTER TRICKED

Dis possum I's et didn' have no scuse
To be beat at his own ol' trick."

BE SHAME!

Little baby, wut you see?
   If you knowed,
You could n' tell; you never is
   Done more 'n crowed.

I 'd be shame', I would,
   To look so wise,
Bein' solemn, den er-smilin'
   Wid my eyes.

If I wus you, you baby,
   I 'd be shame'
To look at supp'n' wut I did n'
   Know its name!

A DREAM OF YOU

Into my fevered brain,
  My hot, unhappy blood,
Like showers of summer rain
  Upon a thirsty wood,
Fair as the first far cloud
  Adrift in April's blue,
There came, white clad and beauty browed,
  A dream of you.

A heaven song sung on earth;
  A vision deserts know,
Mocking their weary dearth,
  Of glades where roses blow.
But day-dawn came and wept,
  A wet wind wailed and blew.
Would I had never waked; had kept
  My dream of you!

LYRICS FROM COTTON LAND

'T was a vandal-hearted fate
  That willed that I should see,
Standing without the gate,
  Life as life could be.
'T was a cruel dawn that brought
  Tidings so falsely true,
That the heaven that smiled was only a
    thought
  A dream of you

ENVIRONMENT

Ol' bull, you pawed de dus' ontil
    It settled on yo' back.
You bellered 'cross de grassy hill,
    En yurlin's cl'ared yo' track.
You hooked de clayroot 'ca'se 't wus red,
    En you could n' stan' fer dat.
You had big notions in yo' head:
    'T wus spring, en you wus fat.

But now yo' back 's bowed, en yo' ha'r
    'S er-standin' up on een'.
It 's dead grass, dead grass ever'whar,
    But not a tussick green.
You disremembers how you run
    When I went atter you,
En how I sweated in de sun,
    En how you sholy flew.

LYRICS FROM COTTON LAND

Oh, you kin stan' behin' dat stack
   En nibble at de straw,
But d' ain't no dus' upon yo' back;
   You do' know how to paw.
You could n' beller now, ner run;
   You 's glad enough to stan'.
'T wus grass en water en hot sun
   Wut made you sich a man.

'POSSUM TIME AGAIN

Oh, dip some 'taters down in grease
En fling de dogs a 'tater apiece.
Ram yo' brogans clean er tacks,
Split de splinters en fetch de ax.
    It 's 'possum time again!

Catfish tender, catfish tough,
We 's done et catfish long enough.
We 's tar'd er collards en white-side meat,
En we 's gwine have supp'n' wut 's good to eat.
    It 's 'possum time again!

De pot 's gwine simmer en blubber en bile
Till it gits scummed over wid 'possum ile.
But le' 's don't brag till we gits de goods.
Whoop! Come along, boys! We 's off to de woods.
    It 's 'possum time again!

NOAH'S ARK

I 's studied all 'bout No-y's ark,
    Its len'th en width en height;
I 's laid awake en studied
    En dremp er it at night:
En how dem three boys wut he had
    Could feed up all dat stock
Beats me, 'ca'se six mules eats enough
    Er cawn fer me to shuck.

Deir women mus' 'a' holp 'em some,
    'Twix' scourin's en 'tween meals,
Er else dem mules en hogs en goats
    'U'd been as lean as eels;
En all dem hosses, deers, en sheeps,
    En ever' cow en kef,
En all de geese en gawslin's would
    'A' perished slam to def.

NOAH'S ARK

Den, when de flood dry up en quit
   En de summer drouf come on
En No-y turnt dem cattle out
   En all de grass wus gone,
How come dey kep' deirse'ves alive?
   'Ca'se all dey lak'd to eat
Wus drownded fust, en den 't wus pahched
   Wid overhettin' heat.

Dar ain't no way, at dis late day,
   To tell how many died
En never took no part at all
   When de yeth wus multiplied.
If all de beasties in dat ark
   Had 'a' come out safe en soun'
Dar 'd be too many in de worl'
   Fer de grass to go aroun'.

Dem animills de circus brings
   Civers all forms en shapes
Dat any man kin think about,

LYRICS FROM COTTON LAND

Zebus, bucks, en apes;
But dey ain't half as many as
   Dar prob'bly mought be er 'm
If No-y 'd had as much good hay
   As he had water fer 'm.

But I turns over in my bed
   En dreams anudder mess,
En wut de answer to it is
   Dan'l he couldn' guess:
I dreams how No-y could 'a' fed
   Dem beasties wut won't eat
No hay ner dough ner grass ner cawn
   Ner anything but meat.

Dar wa'n't but seven rabbits dar:
   One for each fox wus all.
De seven frogs mus' look out whar
   Dem seven snakes gwine crawl.
En dat ol' rooster en his hen
   Dey had to tote de mail

NOAH'S ARK

When seven hongry foxes smelt
   De sweetness er deir trail.

Yas, bruddern, I can't figger why
   Marse No-y's tabby cat
Didn' eat up all de birds dar wus
   Dis side er Ararat;
En, if dem cages wa'n't right strong,
   I would 'a' made a guess
Dat, 'fo' dey landed, one big b'ar
   Would 'a' et up all de res'.

Oh, man, dat wus a roarin' time!
   It wus a rowdy house:
Dem hongry lines could smell, nex' cage,
   'Possums en sheeps en cows;
Dem tigers dey could smell de hens
   En ducks en drakes en geese,
En, if dey growed savygus, dat
   Wus natchel fer a beas'.

LYRICS FROM COTTON LAND

You chillun, hongry as you is
    Fer dis here picnic dinner,
'Long side er dem 'ar wolves, 'u'd be
    Jis' a bran new beginner;
You had yo' brekkus, but dem wolves,
    Wut No-y 's boun' to hyur,
Wus howlin', 'ca'se dey hadn' had
    Nothin' in half a yur.

En den dem varmints wut wus clean
    Had seven fer ever' rout:
One male er one shemale, fer sho,
    Wus boun' to be lef' out.
En when dey come to makin' love
    Dar mus' 'a' been some hate,
'Ca'se ever' time dey counted off
    One didn' have no mate.

En, finely, bruddern, 't wa'n't so bad
    Dat dey wus in de dark
(Dar wa'n't but one li'l' winder, chile,

NOAH'S ARK

In all dat gre't big ark)
So when dey fell to fightin', dey
   Could n' tell which way to go;
Dey had to sniff en listen good
   En move oncommon slow.

En when I studies 'bout dem days
   En thinks upon dat flood,
I 's happy, seein' a rainbow,
   As a cow wut chaws her cud.
En if I 'd been Marse No-y,
   En mought 'a' had my wish,
I 'd 'a' dove fum out dat winder
   En swum off wid de fish.

A MONOLOGUE

De 'possum up de tree
He sot en look' at me,
En when I got de moon 'twix' me en him,
Says I to him, "So, so!
Oh, I 's comin' up, you know,
En I 's gwine a yank you loose fum dat 'ar limb!"

Says I, "Don't putt on airs.
You better say yo' prayers.
De preacher 's gwine be wid me Saddy night,
En he 's glad to eat a 'possum
As a gal to git a blossom,
En his mouf is big en, gosh! his teef is white!"

DE THREE FROSTIES

De fus' fros' browns de simmons,
   En gits de cur dogs fat,
En purples up de simmon leaves
   To show whar dey is at.

De nex' fros' gits de 'possum
   Big en fit to eat:
It fills his hide wid simmon juice
   En greases up his meat.

But 't ain't until de third fros'
   De nigger 'gins to roam,
En takes his torch en cur en ax
   En fetch dat 'possum home.

PUNISHMENT

I LAKS to go to coht en see
Dem lawyers scrappin' all fer me.
Dat big jedge, wid de preacher look,
Readin' in dat-ar yaller book,
Dem twelve big juries, listenin' close
To how I broke ol' Davy's nose,
En all dese people wut you see,
Dey 's all in here beca'se er me.

If I gits out, de gals is mine;
Dey laks a man kin cut a shine.
If I gits in, dey 'll feed me free,
En keep me warm, en let me be
As fat en lazy as I kin.
I kinder hope dey 'll putt me in.

OBEDIENCE

Min' yo' ol' mammy, chilluns,
  Smokin' in de do'!
Don't be mean, now, since she **can't**
  Outrun you any mo'.

WEATHER SIGNALS

When I want to know if it 's gwine a snow,
    I calls my Sambo in.
If he 's kinder scaly 'bout de legs
    En ashy on his chin,
If his hide bees rough lak redoak bark,
    Checked off 'n a reg'lar row,
Sometime 'twix' dat en de fall er dark
    Dar 's gwine a spit some snow.

UTOPIA

When I gits rich I means to use
Whar de mule he hatter have some scuse
Fer lookin' sad; whar de tomcat own
Dese hot still nights a megaphone;
Whar de billygoat, whuruver he goes,
Totes a hanksher fer to blow his nose;
Whar de fice gits paid a ration er meat
Fer ketchin' things wut he won't eat;
En whar, when a man make' up to a gal,
She kin take her ch'ice er go to jail.

THE RACCOON

If wut you want is a' easy snap,
   A 'coon can't he'p you none,
Less'n you ketch him in a trap
   Er kill him wid yo' gun.
All he needs is a fightin' chance,
En he 'll make you pray fer leather pants
En 'll lead yo' cur-dog sich a dance
   Dat he 's glad when he gits done.

He 's little, but, Lawd! he got de san'.
   When you is laid him out,
You needs a stick to he'p you stan',
   'Ca'se yo' head bees whirlin' 'bout.
Oh, his fur is warm en his tas'e is sweet,
But he makes you pay fer his hide en meat;
Whar he bites wid 's mouf er claws wid 's feet
   Yo' blood is gwine a spout.

THE RACCOON

"YO' HEAD BEES WHIRLIN' 'BOUT"

THE CROW'S SHADOW

The crow flew high through the summer sky,
   But a mute and tireless hound,
O'er the meadow-sweeps and up the steeps,
   His shadow, skimmed the ground.

However so high he climbed in the sky,
   O'er river and wood and town,
That shade that crept where the wide earth slept
   Followed and drew him down.

Like a deathless hate or a pitiless fate,
   Like the love of Moab's Ruth,
Or the smouldering fire of an old desire,
   Or the sin of a reckless youth,

THE CROW'S SHADOW

Wherever he went till his life was spent,
   In cloud or in forest dim,
It chased where he led, and where he fell dead
   It was waiting to die with him.

IN A CANOE

The curious current wanders wide
Its guardian swamps from side to side
And mirrors dimly in its tide
    The leafless arch,
Through which, with herald trumpet, stride
    The winds of March.

When, 'twixt-whiles, they forego their stress,
There falls a vasty loneliness,
Such as some city might impress
    On pilgrim hearts,
Where a gray hush holds in duress
    Deserted marts.

IN A CANOE

Then, lo, a feathery tinge of green
About yon willow, faintly seen;
And, where those gnarly maples lean,
    Lo, lightly spread,
Spring's gossamer, a woven sheen
      Of passionate red!

And yonder, those bare limbs among,
Red as the rose that blooms ere long,
The cardinal sits, his bird-heart strong
    With joy refound,
Himself a blaze of light, his song
      A blaze of sound.

Now, when the winds once more take wing,
The great trees shout and groan and swing
The reedy brakes go whispering
    Of seasons fair,
And in my heart the thrill of spring
      Where dead thoughts were,

Till wind and rippling stream and bird
Sing to my pulse in monochord,
And all their song is one wild word:
    "New! new!"—
New hope, fresh purpose, dreams new-stirred,
    And skies all blue!

NAMING THE ANIMALS

When Adam wus namin' de beasties en birds,
   De insexes, fishes, en snakes,
Dey come along pas' him in droves en in herds,
En it took turble thinkin' to think up dem words—
   Mules, elephants, yethworms, en drakes.

How you reckin he come to say lizzud, en fox,
   En tarpin, en buzzud, en bee,
En hoss, en bull-sparrow, en cuckroach, en ox,
En 'possums, en coons, en chickens, en hawks,
   En tiger, en catbird, en flea?

He didn' have time den to study en spit;
   He had to keep 'long wid de game.
He had to putt up wid de bes' he could git.
Wutuver wus passin' he had to name it
   Right dar in its tracks wid a name.

Jis' mule don't mean nothin', ner jackdaw ner mink
  Ner moccasin, rabbit, ner dog;
En him en Miss Eve didn' have time to think.
En dey didn' have time den to eat er to drink
  Er even set down on a log.

But dey done purty well. You try it en see.
  It 's hahd to name even a blossom.
Yit wut could you call a bee but a bee?
'N' if you sees a 'possum way up in a tree,
  You can't think er nothin' but 'possum.

THE RED SHIRTS*

I LAKS red watermillions wut 's juices' when dey
 's red,
I laks red hankshers, washin' days, aroun' my
 ooman's head,
I laks to shuck de red yur, en red lemonade goes
 good,
De Lawd he sot gre't sto' by red in fillin' me wid
 blood;
But when I sees a red shirt, folks, right den is
 when I hushes
En reaches up en gits my hat en totes it to de
 bushes.

En dat 's de way it allus is: de coon he travels
 roun'

---

*Disfranchisement in North Carolina, 1898.

En gits a drink to he'p 'im up, but de drink it
    th'ows 'im down;
He gits a wife to do de work about his little fahm,
But she 's so triflin' in her ways she natchly doos
    him hahm;
En 'ca'se de nigger laks red things—even red ile
    in his lamp—
De white man gits a red shirt fer to make him
    quit de camp.

POOR OLD BEN

Light my pipe en lemme smoke
Nigh de far er pine en oak.
   I 's so ol' en po'ly.
Chillun, I is seed a heap;
It 's 'bout time I gwine to sleep,
   'Ca'se I needs it, sholy.

Dis ol' nigger 's done his shur.
He done shuck' his las' red yur,
   Weighed up his las' cotton.
Now he 's bit wid rheumatiz;
When he walks you sees he is
   Hamstrung en hip-shotten.

Stick a shingle at his head.
Write on it dat Ben is dead,
  Den, in hot er col' times,
Mistis see it, en she say,
"Po' ol' Ben!"—jis' dat a-way,
  Thinkin' er de ol' times.

FOR CORN SHUCKINGS

Oh, come along, come along, Mandy gal!
   I 's a gwine off many a mile.
Did a rainbow ever do you wrong?
   Did a catfish ever smile?

It snowed all night dat hot June day,
   En I says to my gal, say I,
"Oh, gal," says I, en I says, "Oh, gal,"
   En den I pass on by.

De apple tree bloom in de winter time,
   En de leaves shed in de spring,
En all I wants is a little rhyme
   To go wid my banjer string.

ONE DAY

Silent and high a gray hawk wheeled.
Noise of the city, song of the field
Mingled and mellowed their music in one.
Low in the zodiac circled the sun.

Over the valleys the morning was fair,
Keen with the tingle of frost in the air;
Over the mountains a dim mist hung,
Veiling the slow hills, rung by rung.

Faint was the laughter of children at play;
Bells in the meadow seemed far, far away;
Happy the voices of maidens that met:
Oh, 't was a season to hope and forget!

ONE DAY

I had not changed, if I had been God,
One shrouded mountain, one goldenrod,
Where, in his halcyon garment, gold-spun,
Low through the zodiac circled the sun.

A HINDRANCE

You need n' do nothin' but roll in de dirt.
I 'll give you yo' eatin' en give you yo' shirt.
I don't speck yo' he'p when I 's hoein' our farm.
You kin do wut you please, *if you 'll quit doin' harm.*
Why 'n't you sleep in de shade at de eend er de row?
I 'd as well go on home en hang up my hoe,
If you 's gwine a scramble en crawl on de groun'
En roll on de cotton en mash it all down.
Stay whar I putt you! Don't foller my trail!
You mus' 'pen' on dis crap fer yo' winter shirt-tail.
If it 's me dat mus' feed you en give you yo' clothes,
You mus' stay whar I tells you en play wid yo' toes.

A HINDRANCE

"STAY WHAR I TELLS YOU, EN PLAY WID YO' TOES"

A PALLET SLEEPER

I wish a man had a turnin' bed,
'Ca'se he roasties his feet en freezes his head.
When he gits all wrop' up in his civer
He can't turn roun' en he won't turn over.

Dat big far keep on gwine all night
(You kin tell dat fum de chinks bein' bright)
En de heat fum de far en de win' fum de hole
Keeps one een' hot en de udder een' col'.

SUBSTITUTES

We ain't gwine have no turkey
   Less'n we kills him wil',
But we 'll have a pot er cooter soup
   Scum' over wid cooter ile.

We ain't gwine have no poun' cake
   When dat Chris'mas dinner come,
But 'll eat dat cracklin' bread all up
   En hunt anudder crumb.

We mought not have no liquor
   To make us dance aroun',
But 'simmon beer goes purty good
   Atter it settles down.

LYRICS FROM COTTON LAND

In case we don't have powder,
   We won't give up our fun:
We 'll slam a plank ag'in' de groun'
   Loud as a Chris'mas gun.

We all won't go er-huntin'.
   We 'll save our shot en caps,
En 'pen' fer all de birds we gits
   Upon our peckridge traps.

We got no hoss to travel wid,
   But we got a kyart en bull,
En dat 's enough, Gord bless yo' soul
   Fer all we haves to pull.

Oh, folks is fools to cry en cuss,
   'Ca'se deir ves' ain't red en blue!
If you ain't got de spohtin' goods,
   De homespun goods 'll do.

BEDTIME

A PEDDLER travelin' late wus cotch
  Out in a turble rain
Wut sont him runnin' to a house
  Up a long straggly lane.
He did n' know dat house wus whar
  Somebody 'd kilt a man;
He did n' 'spicion ha'nts in dar.
  Oh, my! Oh, my lan'!

He laid down on dat shanty flo',
  Er-listenin' at de rain,
But purty soon he hyeard supp'n' else,
  But he did n' hear it plain.
En den it sounded louder, so
  He 's boun' to onnerstan'
A ghos' wus edgin' up on him,
  Oh, my! Oh, my lan'!

Don't you be feared to go to sleep.
   Now, honey, be a man!
Dat 's right, den—civer up yo' head.
   But, my! Oh, my lan'!

He laid dar, listenin' all he could
   En nigh 'bout scared to def.
Dat ha'nt crope up, en crope so close
   Dat he could feel its bref.
En den he felt supp'n' reachin' roun'
   Lak a graveyardy han';
Dat peddler could n' speak er move.
   Oh, my! Oh, my lan'!

Now, honey, run en hop in bed.
   I ain't gwine tell no mo'
Wut happen to dat lonesome man
   Er-shiverin' on dat flo'.

THE PERSIMMON TREE

De simmon tree is de only tree
   'T ain't cut when de woods is cl'ar'd.
It 's de only shade in de cotton patch
   Fer a man wut 's hot en tar'd.

It 's de only tree wut make a man
   As good as a yaller cur;
Fer a man kin slip aroun' at night
   Fum one tree to an'er.

En treckly th'ow his eye up one
   En look up it a minute,
En way up hyander, 'twix' de moon,
   He see a possum in it.

LYRICS FROM COTTON LAND

It 's de place to lay yo' chillun at
  So dey won't keep a-cryin';
It 's de place to spread yo' cotton sheet
  To save de dew fum dryin'.

De cider piggin sets dar cool,
  Wid yaller bubbles crusted,
En de dog-day watermillion know
  Dat 's whar it gwine be busted.

De sheep scratch off his wool on it,
  En de sow chafe off her mud,
En, dinnertime, de cows comes dar
  To lay en chaw deir cud.

If 't wa'n't fer it you could n' git
  No simmon beer to drink,
Ner fin' no simmon wut you eats
  When its sweet hide 'gins to swink;

THE PERSIMMON TREE

Acorns 'u'd be de shoat's bes' chance;
   De cur 'd be skin en bones;
En de fiel's 'u'd be as b'ilin' hot
   As dem dar horrid zones.

How come dey leaves it on de fahm
   Amongs' de cawn en sich,
It natchly don't eat up de lan'
   But makes it sandbed rich.

En atter it bees dead en gone
   En all de stump done rotten,
Right dar you 'll fin' de heavy cawn
   En de thickes'-fruited cotton.

So when yo' furrow take you pas'
   A simmon somewhar down it,
Nemmine if you does leave some grass,
   You swing yo' plow clean roun' it.

"BELIEVING WHERE WE CANNOT PROVE"

Among the earliest memories that linger in my heart
Is one of old Aunt Phibby Ann, who drew me far apart
And told me, so mysteriously I thought I must have sinned,
That, though it ain't ingenly known, a sow can see the wind.

The wind is mostly blue, she said, but sometimes green or red,
And that is how a sow can tell the weather on ahead.
But a mist has always dimmed my thought—a mist that never thinned—
It being how old Aunt Phibby knew a sow can see the wind.

CONVENIENT THEOLOGY

    I ALLUS has a feelin',
    When I hears a fiddle squealin'
En a banjer-picker pickin' off de time,
    If de chu'ch do stan' ag'in' it,
    Dat dar ain't much danger in it,
En dat cloggin' ain't no sich a turble crime.

    When de gals' heels gits to tappin'
    En de coons gits down to clappin',
Den's when I clogs beca'se—oh, 'ca'se I must!
    Till de tin pans gits to shakin'
    En de flo' boa'ds gits to quakin'
En de far look dim to see it thoo de dust.

LYRICS FROM COTTON LAND

De Lawd he laks good niggers,
Whahfo', here is how I figgers:
I knows de Lawd 'll do wutever 's good;
He made me, heel to noggin;
If dar wus much hahm in cloggin'
He never would 'a' putt it in my blood.

BABY'S NOGGIN

It do look lak we 'd all be dead
When you feels de top er a baby's head.
De sides 'r 'is noggin don't come nigh meetin',
En way up dar his pulse is beatin'.

Jis' s'pose supp'n' shahp 'u'd fall on dar:
It 'u'd be jis' lak thone water on far.
Er s'pose supp'n' heavy 'u'd drap on his head:
You could n' say Scat 'fo' he 'd be dead.

His noggin 's jis' bones, but his brains dey grows,
En I wants to ax if you all knows
Why de brains, since dey got de runnin' start,
Don't prize dat openin' fudder apart?

BLACK MOLASSES

Cawn bread en black molasses
Is better dan honey en hash
    Fer de fahm-han' coon
    En de light quadroon,
Along wid de po' white trash.

You pours it out fum de jug, lak dis;
You sops it up fum de pan.
    En it bees so good
    It he'ps yo' blood
En makes you much of a man.

It 's better wid cooter gravy,
En buttermilk he'ps it some,
    En a piece er catfish
    On de side er de dish
Feels good 'twix' yo' finger en thumb.

BLACK MOLASSES

But jis' de bread en de 'lasses,
Widout any doin' en dash,
    Is enough fer de coon
    En de light quadroon.
En enough fer de po' white trash.

OLD AUNT PLEASANT

Long time 'fo' you wus bawn
   My mistis wus yo' ma.
En now you 's grown en gone,
   En I mus' call you "sah."

Wut 's dat? Jis' call you "honey?"
   Huh! you 's got rich so fas',
Wid lan' en stock en money,
   Dat name 'u'd soun' lak sass.

Nemmin', I holp yo' ma, chile,
   To fix en primp en dress,
En it nuver took me no long while
   To make her look her bes'.

OLD AUNT PLEASANT

Den I 'd stan' at de winder pane,
    A-lookin' out en hummin';
En mistis say, "Kin you see de lane?
    Pleasant, ain't he comin'?"

She meant yo' pa. 'T wa'n't nuver long
    Till 'e rid up, flashin' fine,
En den 't 'u'd 'a' made you sing a song
    To 'a' seed yo' ma's eyes shine.

I holp her on her weddin' night
    Put on her weddin' clothes;
Fum head to heel dem clothes wus white,
    But her cheek was lak a rose.

I jis' do' know how long it 's been.
    Wut, guess? I do' know how.
But I knows dat my young mistis den
    Is my ol' mistis now.

LYRICS FROM COTTON LAND

Law bless de chile! Dat 's lak ol' times!
  Ho much is dis here money?
Dis here 's a half a pint er dimes.
  Now! I *will* call you honey!

THE CROWN OF POWER

De rooster 's crowed, de big bell 's rung.
   Git outen de bed, ol' lady!
Roll outen de bed, en hol' yo' tongue,
En fry dat white-side wut I brung,
   En git my brekkus ready.

Bill, git up fum yo' pallet dar!
   Stick yo' leg into yo' britches,
En when you is kandled up a far,
Go grub till brekkus hyander whar
   De briers is took de ditches.

Sal, you is triflin' fit to kill,
   En foolish as a sheep.
Go fetch some light'ood fum de hill.
Now, all you little coons keep still
   En lemme ketch some sleep.

THE REJECTED SCOTSMAN

I. REJECTED

Hoot! Ye say ye winna hae me, woman?
A Hielandman, right frae the banks o' Lomon'!
Sayin' I 'm rough, that hair shocks oot my ears,
That hair hings o'er my een, my hands jist bear's,
Hairy, hairy a', lak the fiend, an' rough.
Haud, woman! Say na mair, haein' said enough.

Lang hae I looked across the starmy sea,
Thinkin' Amariky was ca'in' me,
O' a' her w'alth an' how her lassies dear
Had lairdly acres, herds, an' mickle gear,
An' how sae kind they wair, sae finely weeded,
An' how a Hielandman was a' they needed.

THE REJECTED SCOTSMAN

Woman, ye ken na what I am.
Nae sark-tailed shepherd wi' 'is yowe an' ram:
Frae an auld stock I spring that spilt mair blood
Than coursed your daddies' veins since No-y's flood.
Ye need na turn, an' shake, an' dry your ee:
Na woman will I hae winna hae me!

2. TOLD ON

The hizzy might hae kep' it tae hersel'.
Sae prood she was she could na hellup but tell;
An' now frae her big braggin' comes to pass
'T is kenned by effery ither village lass,
Wha, when they see me comin', squeak an' say,

"I want na man wham ithers wadna hae!"
Weel, gang your ways, ye little gigglin' sillies,
An' wed, God rest ye, wi' your ain town billies
(Pale little lads, wham I could mak' tae mind me
An' whip them a' wi' one hand tied behind me),
An' brag tae them abou' the honest man,

Frae wham, for their slim sakes, ye squeaked **an'**
    ran.

Tauld it, yiss! an' may a' ill befa' me
If "h'isted Scotsman" isna what they ca' me!
I 'll hae it on them: in my ain countrie
Ilk lass wad die tae gang tae kirk wi' me;
An' there I 'll wed some chieftain's sprightly
    daughter—
If this deil's-gossip comes na o'er the water!

3. COALS OF FIRE

Whist, Peggy, woman! Pass these houses here
Bonny an' prood an' spry, wi' mickle cheer;
Look at me sae, an' smile intil my face—
Look lovin', if it be God gies ye grace;
Nar fear I wad your winsome passion check
If ye sho'd hing your airms abou' my neck!

THE REJECTED SCOTSMAN

(Aside)

Now let the hizzies peep as we gang by,
An' deil a cheek amang them will be dry!
I 'll spraid mysel' an' step wi' lairdly gait,
Stare cauld on Peggy, my unwarthy mate;
I 'll wark my shaulders an bulge oot my chist,
That they may rue the braw man they hae misst.

If ony o' them mark us, or their mithers,
'T winna be lang in gaein' tae the ithers—
How that the "h'isted Scotsman" in his pride
Gaed past them wi' his ain rid-headed bride,
Which canna hellup but burn them tae the bane
(Na kennin' Peg 's a sister o' my ain).

4. ONE SIDE OF IT

It gars me greet how women a' must wait
Until a man comes knockin' at their gate.
Their lives must be sae mirky wi' regret
For the braw men they lo'ed but could na get.

LYRICS FROM COTTON LAND

It is na fair tae mak' them haud their voice
An' never hae the dares tae name their choice.

Ye askit, did ye, why I never wed?
I was na fool enough tae lose my head.
Ah, lad, on baith sides o' the starmy sea
There hae been lassies pined an' died for me—
Bonny sweet lassies ither men fought o'er
An' fared nae better after than before.

Yiss, there be women, auld an' warn an' gray,
Wha wanted me, but could na tell me sae.
'T is weel, nae doot; for it had been unkind
Tae tell them that they did na suit my mind.
Nae Hielandman, bred on the braes o' Lomon',
Wad be sae beastly tae a gentlewoman.

A SOFT SNAP

I 's tar'd er work, I is,
En I 's gwine a shirk my biz.
    I 's a yaller coon,
    En late en soon
I 's gwine a rest, I is.

I 's gwine a teach a while;
En den I 'll preach a while:
    It 's easy teachin'
    En easy preachin',
En I 's gwine a gi' 'm a trīle.

AMBITION

I AIN'T decided what I 'll be.
    It 's sortie hard to tell.
Sometimes I think I 'll go to sea
    An' try the sea a spell.
Sometimes I think I 'll take an' try
    My chances on the lan'.
But anyhow I aim to be
    A mighty turble man.

No; Susie would n' kiss me
    When we played the game o pawn.
An' Billy laughed at my bow legs
    An' ast to try 'em on.
An' Jim sayed I was sunburnt
    Jis' like a Croatan.
They 'll hate this when I git to be
    A mighty turble man.

AMBITION

They 'll come into my palace.
    I 'll be dressed up in silk.
They 'll say, We 're pore an' hungry, sir,
    An' want some buttermilk.
I 'll give 'em wine an' honey,
    An' then I 'll rise an' stan'
An' say, 'T was me you th'owed off on—
    A mighty turble man!

They 'll whimper then, you bet they will,
    An' wish that they was dead.
An' when they git down on their knees,
    Lak kneelin' at yore bed,
An' beg me not to kill 'em, then
    I 'll ketch 'em by the han'
An' say, Don't ever laugh no more
    At a sunburnt, bow-leg man!

THE SIESTA

I TELLS 'em to please
  Bile a dinner er pease
En set me a table out under de trees,
  Den lemme be fed
  Wid a pone er corn bread
En ingerns; den lemme lay down on a bed.

  Oh, de skeeter kin sting
  En de dirt-dauber sing,
De housefly kin tickle my yur wid 'is whing;
  De chillun kin bawl,
  De cuckroach kin crawl
Up my britches, en ganders en peafowls kin
    squall;

THE SIESTA

    Oh, the dishes kin break
    En de shetters kin shake
But all kin er fusses can't keep me awake,
      'Ca'se it takes more 'n dese
      T' onsettle my ease,
When I's et a good dinner er corn-pone en peas.

THE DIEDIPER

De diediper swum on de millpon',
  En de nigger crope roun' de dam,
En cock his gun en took good aim
  En pull de trigger, blam!

But 'fo' de bullets got dar
  De diediper done dove down.
He dove, en dove, en den pop up
  En 'gin to floatin' roun'.

De nigger crope thoo bushes
  Till he got anudder trile.
De diediper dove, en dove, en dove,
  But he pop up atter while.

THE DIEDIPER

So he shot his caps en powder
  En his ramrod, too, away,
But de diediper floats upon dat pon'
  En swims right dar to-day.

SNAKES

De whup-snake drags a platted tail.
He runs as straight as a railroad rail.
  He got no voice, but slick en sof'
He 'll twis' hisse'f aroun' yo' wais',
En lick his col' tongue in yo' face,
  En whup yo' shirt-tail off.

De hoop-snake roll lak a waggin tar.
His horn 'll sting you wuss 'n far.
  But he can't 'pen' on his eyes.
He 'll slam his horn right in some tree,
En dar he 'll stay en dar he 'll be
  Till de tree en him bofe dies.

SNAKES

You hits de j'int-snake in de grass,
En he busties up, jis' same as glass,
   En den you thinks he 's dead;
But 'fo' you goes to mill en back,
He 's done j'ined up, en dar 's his track,
   Whar he cross' de sof' san'-bed.

MYSTERIES

How de flyin' squir'l fly is a wonder to me.
En how a blacksnake kin clamb a tree
    Is a wonder to me.

How a catfish breave I jis' can't tell,
En a chicken, befo' he busties his shell.
    No. I can't tell.

BABY'S LEGS

Babies' legs is allus bowed.
   Deir legs ain't never straight.
Why, mistis, ain't you never knowed
   You can't do nothin' but wait?

He hol's his heels up all de time,
   En p'ints 'em at de sky.
It 's too soon yit fer him to try 'm.
   Dey 'll come right by en by.

GRASS

It 's good de grass is late to sprout
    En gives de cawn some start,
'Ca'se, if dey sprung togedder, dey
    'U'd never tease apart.

De grass is had to fight its way
    Ag'in us all so long,
Dat, fum its reg'lar wras'lin',
    It grows up powerful strong.

It grows so strong dat, if you ups
    En leaves it to itse'f,
Dis grass 'll fight dat udder grass
    Till dey chokes deirse'ves to def.

THE VARMINT CONVENTION

When de varmints hilt deir meetin',
        Honey-loo, honey-loo,
'T wus a long time dey wus greetin' en er-treatin'
        en er-eatin'
'Fo' dey 'cided in dat meetin'
        Wut to do.

Br'er Coon he took a notion,
        Loo-honey, honey-loo,
'T wus his time to make a motion.
        (Chicken, shoo-shoo-shoo.)
"If de motion gwine prevail,
Ever' man jis' raise his tail;
Don't, de motion 's gwine a fail."
        (Hoo-doo, hoo-doo.)

LYRICS FROM COTTON LAND

Br'er Possum grin a little,
        Honey-loo-oo-oo,
En he say it wa'n't de gemman
        Thing to do.
"Br'er Coon know' it ain't fair.
His tail 's got rings en hair,
But mine is slim en bare.
        (Boo-hoo, boo-hoo.)

"More 'n dat, it ain't fair totin',
        Loo-loo, honey-loo.
Marse Goat 's done done his votin'
        'Head er you.
How kin it be fair totin'?
'T ain't nothin' but jis' goatin'.
Marse Bill 's gwine keep on votin'
        Clean thoo." (Oo-oo.)

Wid dat dey falls to fightin',
        Loo-honey, honey-loo.

THE VARMINT CONVENTION

Bless Gord, it wus a sight. 'n'
        Dat is true.
De goat walk up a rail,
Shake his little stubby tail,
En den he tote de mail.
        (Oh, loo-hoo-hoo.)

THE COON FROM THE COLLEGE TOWN

Oh, dress up, ladies, finer 'n you is,
'Ca'se you 's gwine wid a man wut knows his biz.
De cawn-fiel' han' en de cotton-patch nigger,
De laborin' man don't cut no figger,
When it 's Come along, ladies, en foller me roun',
De dead-game spoht fum de college town.

I totes my guitah wid a shoulder strap,
En now en again I gives it a rap,
Er-hummin' ol' chunes fum way down Souf,
Wid a cigaroot rollin' aroun' in my mouf.
I 'd be plum white, if I jis' wa'n't brown,
Fer I feels at home in de college town.

THE COON FROM THE COLLEGE TOWN

I kerries de notes wut 's boun' to go
Fum de boys to de ladies on Faculty row.
Fer singin' at night I gits mo' pay
Dan my ol' man gits fer ploughin' all day.
When dar 's supp'n' to drink, I swallers it down,
'Ca'se I gits wut 's gwine in de college town.

Oh, I gits to look at de ball game free
Fer thone up fouls wut flies toge me,
En de tournament costies me nary a cent,
'Ca'se I sees wut way de tennis balls went.
En dey couldn' git along on de football groun'
If it wa'n't fer de coon fum de college town.

My britches belonged to a rich young man;
My coat 's a jim-swinger en my ves' is tan;
My collar en tie, my shoes en my socks,
When dey fus' wus bought dey costed de rocks.
A spoht by day en at night a clown—
Oh, sich is de life er de college town!

IF

"If I had gold," the ragged plodder said,
"Fame's laurel soon would aureole my head.
For eloquence and beauty in my heart
Lie waiting for the leisure-need of art."

"If I were poor," said he of idle days,
"Then might I gain a people's pride and praise.
But fame shuns fortune, making effort vain.
All greatness grows from poverty and pain."

Oh, patient if! Burdened with all who fail,
Thine is a heart-sore, never-ending tale!
And they who plead thee know the hero's lance
Must brave the armored breast of circumstance.

TOT AND TED

If Tot and Ted would sit up late
Till all the coals died in the grate
And all the house grew still and dark
And Man, the cur, would not dare bark;

If they sat still and bolt awake
And would not leave till broad daybreak,
Their pains would be worth while, because
They'd get to see old Santa Claus.

So fat is he, so small the flue,
'T were nice to know how he gets through
And does not leave a track of soot
About the hearth to mark his foot.

LYRICS FROM COTTON LAND

But Ted and Tot will not sit up.
The sandman and the sleepy cup
Will fill their eyes and drowse them so
They'll fall asleep before they know.

Santa will see them when he comes
Lugging his load of dolls and drums,
And he will smile, as who should say,
"I wish grown folks could sleep that way."

And when he fills their stockings full
Of slings and sweets and things to pull,
He'll look at head and curly head,
And say, "Good-by, old Tot and Ted."

How down the chimney does he squeeze?
How climbs he back with unskint knees?
Don't ask me questions, Ted and Tot:
You watch and see the how and what.

TOT AND TED

If you can stay awake—just so—
From sundown until rooster crow
And watch for Santa's furry hood,
You'll be the first that ever could.

BOYS' VISIONS

S'pose I could fly!
   I bet you I would brag,
Fer not a gal in school could take my tag.
I 'd keep my wings hid till they 'mos' got there
'N' nen I 'd sail up, laughin', in the air,
Danglin' my heels a leetle out o' reach,
An' toss 'em back a biscuit er a peach!

If I could fly,
   I wouldn't go to school,
Ner go to mill a-straddle of no mule.
I 'd jis' sail out an' see what I could fin',
Fer ever'thing I saw, you know, 'd be mine.
Bloodhoun's an' 'tectives jis' 's well go die.
I wouldn't make no tracks, if I could fly.

BOYS' VISIONS

If I could fly,
 I 'd do like Robin Hood,
An' rob the other robbers in the wood.
I 'd run frum them a little ways, right slow,
An' nen I 'd say, "Bye, bye," an' up I 'd go
With all the diamonds what the robbers had.
My! but don't you know 't'u'd make 'em mad!

If I could fly,
 I 'd build a house o' stone,
An' nen I 'd need a wife, when I got grown.
I 'd ast the king to lemme have his gal,
Callin' 'im to 'is face ol' pard an' pal,
An' when he wouldn', I 'd jis' say, "That 's
    tough,"
An' pick the princess up an' tote her off.

If I could fly,
 I 'd buy 'em things at home,
A new stove an' a skillet an' a broom,
A fine horse with a ribbin on his tail,

'N' nen I 'd gittum a new milkin' pail.
I bet I 'd make 'em think an' study some.
Ma 'd say, "Where—do—these—things—come—
    frum?"

HOLDING OFF THE CALF

THEY all 'll tell you I wouldn't mind
   A-holdin' the kef at all
If it didn't come at the very time
   I hear the other boys call.
Jis' when I see 'em a-goin' by
   Wi' their dogs an' guns in a hurry,
An' I want to go, I hear maw cry
   'At she 's ready to milk ol' Cherry!
An' there I stan' wi' the kef by the yur,
   The boys done out o' sight,
An' maw *a-whang, a-whang,* jis' like
   She aimed to take all night.

'Bout sundown 's time for the swimmin'-hole,
   But from me it 's mighty fur:
That 's jis' the minute each blessed day
   I must ketch the kef by the yur.

The parson, my bud—he 's a preacher, you know,
    But he can't git nowhere to preach—
Looks on wi' 's thumbs in 'is gallus straps,
    Smilin' sweet as a peach.
The kef is a fool, don't mean no harm,
    Only wantin' to suck;
But sometimes I git so awful mad
    I twisties his yur like a shuck.

They all say I 'm lazy, no count in the worl',
    Only to raise a row;
But I would n't mind workin' all times o' day
    'Cep' the time for milkin' the cow.
Whenever the fellers go off to swim,
    Along wi' their dogs an' gun,
That pore white kef, a-wantin' his share,
    Heads off both ends o' my fun.
But some sweet day I 'll be a man,
    An' when I 'm boss myse'f,
I 'll ketch ever' boy 'at stays on the place
    An' put him to holdin' a kef!

WHEN THE CALVES GET OUT

I 've run so long I 'm tired to death!
   I 'll have to rest a while.
An' then before I ketch my breath
   They 'll gain about a mile.
They 'll go an' keep on goin',
   'N' oon't never turn about,
For they leave an' hush their lowin',
   When the keves git out.

A cow 's a fool about her kef!
   If she kin steal him off
She 'll lick him an' enjoy herse'f
   Like fresh salt in her trough.
An' when you try to head 'em
   It 's a jangle an' a rout.

They forgit 't wus you 'at fed 'em,
  When the keves git out.

Sis she would never milk too late
  ('F she had to herd the cows)
To try the bars an' latch the gate
  'Fore goin' to the house.
But 't ain't the time for swearin',
  An' 't ain't wuth while to pout;
It 's keep the bell in hearin',
  When the keves git out.

I 'll git some bull to lead the drove,
  An' then I 'll drive 'em slow,
Ease 'em along from grass to grove,
  So they oon't hardly know.
It never does to push 'em
  An' run an' rare an' shout;
You 're losin' time to rush 'em,
  When the keves git out.

CATS

Thar air good p'ints as well as bad, that c'recterizes cats;
Their purrin' sounds so comf'table, and then they ketches rats.
They likes to play with chillun, an' they don't take much to eat,
An' thar 's mighty few housekeepers kin head 'em bein' neat.

An' yit I never see a cat, to study him a spell,
But whut thar comes a feelin' that he's back an' forth frum hell;
An' when he purrs an' rubs my leg an' hides his crooked claws,
Thinks I, Whut split your nose an' yur an' made streaks on your jaws?

He 's gentle 'nough about the hearth whar
    Mandy darns an' knits;
But watch that green light in his eyes when he
    bows his back an' spits!
He stays at home till bedtime comes an' then he
    creeps away:
You 'll see him slippin' back again nex' mornin'
    through the gray.

He 's mighty cosy on the rug, a-lappin' from a
    cup;
But he 's the only daddy that will eat his chillun
    up.
An' when the tabby goes to move, she grabs a
    kitten's head
An' lets him swing an' flop about like he was
    supp'n' dead.

To leave him in the room at night, you know, is
    sartain death;

CATS

He 'll snug right 'mongst the blankets an' suck
    the baby's breath.
I 've been at many a settin'·up with my departed
    kin
Scared half to death to see them cats, like ghos-
    ties, comin' in.

I may be hard upon ol' Tom, but Growler hates
    him, too,
An' when it comes to jedgin' hearts, I think that
    dog will do.
Tom likes an old maid; an' he likes to go out in
    the road
At fall o' dusk an' spend his time a-playin' with
    a toad.

Sometimes I think I 'd like the job o' goin' round
    the yeth
An' puttin' every single cat nine separate times to
    death;

For thar 's a thousand reasons that I won't take
    time to tell
Why I am bound to b'lieve a cat is back an' forth
    frum hell.

TO ALFONSO XIV

LATEST in line of royal sons,
  Pink on your silver platter,
Despite the bugles, flags and guns,
  And courtiers trained to flatter,
You hoist your heels, blink at your toes,
  And smile and stare and blubber,
And are as careless of your clothes
  As any low-born lubber.

Softly! you must not understand,
  You muling, sniffling fellow,
You bear the blood of Ferdinand
  And pious Isabella!
You cannot know the mingled breed
  Of many kingdoms, growing

LYRICS FROM COTTON LAND

In your small shape, the fertile seed
    Of long selected sowing.

When a few years shall give you speech
    And school your legs to bear you,
What precepts will your masters preach
    For kingship to prepare you?—
For fetes and forms and pageantries
    And armies brave with banners,
Till they accomplish your disguise
    And lose a man in manners.

Will they insist on prinks and prigs,
    Or let you romp and lark it
And count your toes for weebit pigs
    A-going all to market?
Will they inform your pate with lore
    And ancient classic schooling,
Or let you read, flat on the floor,
    Old Mother Hubbard's fooling?

TO ALFONSO XIV

'T is not through envy of your state
   Or natural plebean malice,
But could I bribe who guards your gate
   And steal into your palace,
I 'd smuggle you into the woods,
   When oaks are first in tassel,
And let you build, in happy moods,
   Many a Spanish castle.

There you would learn the simple need
   Of laughter, love, and labor,
The common fireside ways, the creed
   That binds one to his neighbor.
But this is idle. I should think
   Of what in reason may be.
So here your royal health I drink,
   You pink, plump, bareleg baby!

A TOMTIT MESSENGER

Above the din the alien sparrows made
  In the city's April shade,
I heard one native note, one tomtit's cry
  Wandering through the sky.

His tune, though calm, was like a bugle call
  From wood and waterfall,
And waked the memories of brooks and springs
  And vines and vernal things.

Faster than his swift wings might drive him there
  My thoughts had traveled where
The oriole, in his gold and sable dressed,
  Sings near his woven nest;

A TOMTIT MESSENGER

Where the wide wood but half foregoes its hush
   For the lyric-throated thrush;
And where the orchards and the arbors thrill
   With the mock-bird's rapturous bill.

Only to courts where nature still is queen,
   What time the year grows green,
These minstrels gather with their varied glee
   To brake and brier and tree,

And leave the city's cornices and spires
   To those discordant choirs
Whose breed some ill-directed eastward breeze
   Blew hither o'er the seas.

To you, you wandering tomtit, for the news
   Of April sounds and hues
And busy joy of all the woodland brood,
   A stranger's gratitude!

TO ONE WHO IS GOOD

A RAINBOW's colors canvas'd on a cloud;
   A lone red rose among the burly briers;
   In winter's chill the glow of friendly fires;
A pitying heart where other hearts are proud:
These are like thee; and like thee, too, the shroud
   Which beauty spreads upon the dying year,
   Or some sweet star that watches, calm and clear,
Above the sea when waves and winds are loud.

I know man's life is sick with sin and grief,
   Which age on age hath not sufficed to cure;
That sorrow lingers long, but joy is brief,
   And creeds change, but the old, old crimes endure:
Which vasty gloom serves but to lend relief
   To thee, for other souls the cynosure.

DEW

I GITS my chillun up 'fo' day,
'Ca'se de dew it makes de cotton weigh.
I feeds 'em on a chance er peas,
I ties de pads upon deir knees,
En 'fo' de day break here we goes,
Draggin' our sacks betwix' de rows.
Dem udder niggers do' know why
My cotton tetch de scales so high.
Dar 's supp'n' wrong dey speck; dey know
Deir famblies gethered row fer row.
But I jis' squints en spits—key-chew!
Is I gwine tell 'em 'bout de dew?

RACE SUICIDE

Old bullbat hen, you made no nest.
With two dull eggs beneath your breast,
Among the clods, yourself a clod,
You sit and see the ploughman plod.

Circling the sunny summer skies,
Now high, now low, your bullbat flies,
And stoops anon from out the blue
To bray his jest of love to you.

Perhaps your heart is happy when
You count your duty done, old hen;
But I would let the bullbat race
Die out, before I'd take your place.

RACE SUICIDE

If I were you, I would not see
My bullbat swoop and laugh at me,
Nor be content, along the grass,
To see his errant shadow pass;

But by his side, with wings as good,
I'd bask in drifting altitude,
Bellow at clouds and browsing sheep,
And lull my dust-desires to sleep.

THE FIRST FLOWER

Under the leaves on the south of the hill,
Where the wind and the winter have wasted their
 will
And the pale grass whispers and blinks in the sun,
The season of seven sweet moons is begun;

The season of seven fair crescents and crowns,
Ere the frost and the autumn's slow fruitage em-
 browns
The green and the crimson, the gold and the
 gloom
Of woods where the first flower is waked into
 bloom.

For the first flower is prophet of all that was
 dreams,

THE FIRST FLOWER

The dappled lane-shadows, the ripple of streams,
The old hope and love that so lately were young,
And the old song that waits once again to be sung.

Ah, would that the last flower might bloom to
    fulfill
The pledge of this first on the south of the hill!
And would the last moon might incline to its slope
In memory as sweet as this first is in hope!

DEAD

THEY spoke sweet words above her bier
   Of some all-happy shore,
Where no pain comes to cause a tear
   Ever and evermore;
They made a garden of her grave,
   Where many a fair vine creeps,
And to her tomb this comfort gave:
   "She is not dead; she sleeps."

They told me birds would come to sing
   For her a lullaby;
That for her sake the stars would swing
   Their watch-fires through the sky;
That conscious winds would will to stir
   The roses at her head,

DEAD

And all the suns would dawn for her,
  Who sleeps, and is not dead.

They said her spirit loves me still,
  Sees all, and understands.
But where the lips that spoke her will—
  Where are her eyes and hands?
Not all men's prayer that she should live
  Can move the guard of death,
Nor all the lore of ages give
  Her little body breath.

The birds may sing, the flowers may start
  Each spring where old flowers were,
But I can never teach my heart
  That they bear heed to her.
Nor my fond passion to disguise
  With light the path I grope
Can give me back her love-lit eyes,
  Her heart-beat, and my hope.

LYRICS FROM COTTON LAND

I know so little! It is strange
   A flower should be cut down,
Ere, with its mates, it suffered change
   To autumn's gradual brown.
But this I know: should I grow old
   Beyond the years of men,
I shall not ever, ever hold
   My arms for her again.

VIEWPOINTS

Down in his dusty cellar place,
   On a stool of triple legs,
The apron'd cobbler sits and drives
   His gleaming row of pegs.

High in his sunlit window nook,
   Above the rumbling mart,
The poet stares across the hills
   And meditates his art.

That each bemoans the other's lot
   Is natural human pride;
For the cobbler sees one side of life,
   And the bard the other side.

OLD JIM SWINK

THEY tell me old Jim Swink is dead
   And buried 'neath the bough
Of that big cedar in the field
   Where he was wont to plough.
He liked to sit within that shade
   To cool a bit and think
That all the land he saw belonged
   To old Jim Swink.

He made me many a pebble-sling
   And many a locust bow,
And I would take him water
   To his grassy turning row
And watch his Adam's-apple move,
   The while he stood to drink,

OLD JIM SWINK

Up and down the leathery neck
  Of old Jim Swink.

We shared our rabbit boxes,
  Our powder, shot, and caps.
We fared through many a frosty dawn
  To our deadfalls and our traps,
And ofttimes found in waiting
  A muskrat, coon, or mink.
He was as much a child as I,
  Was old Jim Swink.

The cedar berries cluster blue,
  The cedar birds are gay
Amid the bossy boughs that shade
  The old man's dust to-day.
He knows no times and seasons now,
  No suns will rise and sink,
No change of moon suggest his toil
  To old Jim Swink.

LYRICS FROM COTTON LAND

I do not wish to sing for him
    A song of curious art;
This song would be more sweet to him,
    Simple as was his heart.
He would be glad if he could know
    How tenderly I think
Of those wild, rough, go-lucky days
    With old Jim Swink.

THE DOODLE BUG

Under a log propped high enough to leave a
 sheltered place
The doodle bug he delves his home and propa-
 gates his race.
He delves it in the doodle dust and makes it very
 cavey
That every ant that blunders in may be his meat
 and gravy.

*Here I draw a tickle straw. Linkum, tinkum,
 tire.*
Come up, doodle, doodle bug! Your house is afire.

The doodle feels the doodle dust cave down where
 he is hid.

LYRICS FROM COTTON LAND

He thinks an ant's feet must have done what my
    pine needle did.
He bulges through his powdery floor and jerks
    himself around,
And then is when I lay him out upon the solid
    ground.

Weed 'll do; needle, too; willow wand, or wire.
Come up, doodle, doodle bug! Your house is
    afire.

You need n't use a straw at all, but blow into his
    home,
And, yicky, yecky, yerky, jerky, up that bug will
    come.
No bones, no blood, no hair or heels, no tail, no
    tools for strife,
A little ball of rubber he, electrified with life.

THE DOODLE BUG

*Woe and death; blow your breath; run here and
    respire.*
Doodle, doodle, doodle bug, your house is afire.

And why the good Lord made him I cannot figure
    out.
There's nothing to him but his shape and his
    two-horned snout.
And how he gets from place to place is more than
    I can tell,
But where the doodle dust invites the doodle bug
    doth dwell.

Yinky yanky, snicky snacky. Jerk until you tire.
Doodle bug, O doodle bug! Your house is afire.

Perhaps who made the roses sweet and made the
    blue sky fair
That weary human hearts might find surcease of
    toil and care

Designed this dusty delver, this petty beast of
    prey,
That children might be happier with one more
    game to play.

Doodle bug, oodle ug, irky, icky, ire.
Come up to the surface, lad! Your house is afire.

AUTUMN

Heavy with sleep is the old farmstead;
   The windfall of orchards is mellow;
The green of the gum tree is shot with red,
   The poplar is sprinkled with yellow.
Sluggish the snake and leafy the stream;
   The fieldmouse is fat in his burrow;
Sun-up sets millions of dewdrops a-gleam
   Where the late grass is grown in the furrow.

Oh, the smell of the fennel is autumn's own breath,
   And the sumac is dyed in her blood;
The charr of the locust is what her voice saith,
   And the cricket is one with her mood.
Soft are her arms as soft-seeded grass,
   The bluebells at dawn are her eyes,

And slow as slow winds are her feet as they pass
    Her bees and her butterflies.

And when I grow sick at man's sorrow and crime,
    At the pain on pale womanly faces,
At the fever that frets every heart-throb of time,
    At all that brings grief or debases,
I thank God the world is as wide as it is,
    That 't is sweet still to hope and remember;
That, for him who will seek them, the valleys are
        his
    And the far quiet hills of September.

THE THREE TOTS

Three tots went out in the early days
   To see what spring had done.
"Let 's find us flowers along the ways
   Most like the spring," said one.
"Let 's find a flower of sky-like blue,
A flower that for the clouds will do,
And a flower of such a golden hue
   It well might be the sun."

One found a crocus, for the sky;
   And one found, bright and bold,
A dogwood, white as clouds on high,—
   More clouds than three could hold;
And one went far to woodland ways
And found a jasmine's torch a-blaze.
So were complete the early days:
   Sapphire, silver, gold.

"Would we could meet with Spring," said
  one.
  "Her garden grew these flowers;
This crocus-sky, this jasmine-sun,
  These clouds for petal showers.
'T is not long since she 's been this way.
She 's wandering in these woods to-day.
How she 'd be pleased to watch us play
  This game of hers and ours!"

AT THE DANCE

SHE seemed to watch the dancers pass
  And listen to the thrill
Of flutes and strings that swelled and sank
  As they had had one will.
She seemed to see and hear and mark
  Each moment's fall and rise.
Why else that bright rose in her cheek,
  That great light in her eyes?

She did not turn about to meet
  His gaze who whispered near;
Save for the flutter of her hands,
  She seemed not even to hear.
She did not part her lips to speak
  A single answering word,
But there were they who saw her throat
  Quiver, and knew she heard.

And there were they who knew her cheek
  Bloomed not from music's art;
The lustre in her waking eyes
  Could burn but from her heart;
The sinuous sounds and lissom steps
  About the lighted hall
Faintly upon her senses fell
  As the shadows on the wall.

Hither and thither went the throng;
  Laughter and life ran high;
Gay youth and girlhood passed and took
  The smell of roses by.
She was not conscious that they lived;
  Amid their rounds of mirth
(Save for his presence at her side)
  She was alone on earth.

It was a blessed hour for her;
  For them a blessed hour
Who saw her woman's heart unfold

AT THE DANCE

As it had been a flower;
Who saw a new light in her eyes
 Kindle and grow to dawn—
The light that none in heaven, and few
 On earth may look upon.

And they who saw and understood
 Knew hardly what they felt:
It was as if at some new shrine
 Of beauty they had knelt
And shared the wonder of a joy
 Whose wordless lips confess
The height of all high things, the depth
 Of utter tenderness.

"FETCH DAT MILLION ROUN' TO ME"

SELFISHNESS

Dar you is! Dar you is!
   I jis' knowed 't wus you.
Mornin's I is seed yo' trail
   Stragglin' 'cross de dew.
Dat's why I sayed I 'us gwine off,
   When I wa'n't studyin' gwine:
I aimed to watch en see you break
   Dat million fum de vine.
You need n' lie! I *seed* you, boy!
   You need n' try to run;
You need n' hide behin' de house,
   'Ca'se dat won't he'p you none.
But fetch dat million roun' to me.
   I needs dat fruit myse'f.
You stan' right over dar en see
   If any gwine be lef'.

LYRICS FROM COTTON LAND

You thought you 'd eat it all, you did,
   Now, all you 'll git 's de rin'.
I hates dat sich a selfish kid
   Happened to be mine!

DESERTED

She strove to hide
Her heart-break from us ('t was her maiden
    pride)

And as she went
From room to room upon her duty bent

She made gay quips,
Nor could we tell a quiver at her lips.

When all was still
Deep in the night, except one whippoorwill,

We, wakeful yet,
Heard when she sobbed, and knew her cheeks
    were wet.

GRANDADDY-LONG-LEGS

Grandaddy spider,
Spread your legs wider,
Sniff some, and study, and scent,
And show me the way
My cow went to-day,
The way that my milk cow went.

I 'll tickle your back
To give me her track
And to tell where she 's browsing now.
Lift up a foot
And point it, and put
Me straight on the trail o' my cow.

THE CASTLE BUILDER

Come back, tired dreams, across the sea, and rest
   These other years with me,
Like weary migrants to an empty nest
   Where singing used to be.

Tired boyhood dreams, if I had followed you,
   Had done your proud behest,
Had crossed the purple hills that barred my view
   And braved the giant West,

Had sailed the Eastern oceans where your wings
   Flashed white against the blue,
Perhaps they had not been mere shadow kings
   That all our lives we knew,

But Pharaoh's realm and Egypt's wine and corn
    And all men's high esteem,
Had Joseph's courage in my heart been born
    A twin with Joseph's dream.

TO-MORROW

Though sun after sun set on dreams unfulfilled,
    And night after night fall in sorrow,
Faint hope is revived and old courage new-thrilled
    With the promise that beckons to-morrow.

She lures every pilgrim from childhod to age;
    She downs every pillow with pleasure;
To the ill-guided pencil she lends a new page;
    She pilots the poor to her treasure.

The great song for singing, the far height to reach,
    The heart that at last makes confession,
The wisdom that all other days could not teach:
    These are her pledge and possession.

LYRICS FROM COTTON LAND

For some there is faith, for all there is hope,
   When the dark falls behind and before us,
And the sun is no more, we shall not need to grope,
   But shall find her own face dawning o'er us.

A CHOICE

Our senses wake so stupidly
  From the dim dawn of birth,
Become so gradually aware
  Of all that makes the earth,
That, ere we halve our journey,
  Grass and green trees and flowers
Are common things, and even the sun
  But serves to mark the hours.

Would you have chosen, had you known
  And heaven been so content,
To live unconscious of the light,
  Of form and sound and scent,
Until your heart had learned its wish
  And your brain its guided prime:
Then to have had the world burst forth
  All in one pulse of time?

LYRICS FROM COTTON LAND

I think not. When you came to count
    The quiet tale of years,
The friendly welcome for each flower
    Whose season reappears,
The well-trod, unsurprising path
    That leads from dawn to dusk
And on from April's swelling bud
    To winter's empty husk,

I do not think that you would take,
    As worth the loss of these,
A blaze of sudden glory
    That would bring you to your knees;
Nor should I wish to stand in awe
    And worship, what I love,
The old grass cool beneath my feet
    And the old stars calm above.

THE IRON DOOR

WHETHER I gaze into the night
At suns that seem mere points of light,
And, framing metaphors to reach
Through vastness with the art of speech,
I learn that lighted space is wrought
Too wide for even the range of thought;

Or whether in the depths I grope
For monsters of the microscope
That prey and sport, are born and die,
And feel that, 'neath the aided eye,
Life feeds on life, gate leads to gate,
Too deep for thought to penetrate:

How small am I for care or curse
From the Maker of the universe!

How great, above the microsprites,
Thus to be left with broken lights,
Through toil and prayer and pain, to find,
If so I can, the Maker's mind!

Food, that my body may not die;
Love, that my kind may multiply;
Birds and fair blooms, that time flow sweet
Over my head, about my feet:
And farther would I delve or soar
I bruise me at an iron door.

THE TENANT

To die and to live are the nearest of neighbors,
   And death is to life the closest of kin;
Heir to life's harvest of love and her labors,
   The skull waits under the skin.

But while she endures she guards her possession;
   Hers is the key to the citadel locks;
Even the Lord, when he covets admission,
   Stands at the door and knocks.

Patient, O Death, thy reign is hereafter,
   Bide thee thy crowning and keep thee apart!
Mine this estate, this lease upon laughter,
   Mine all the love in my heart.

HORSEMINT

In the calm of summer lanes
   And the hoof-betrodden spaces,
   Idle over-pastured places,
There the dusty horsemint reigns.

Not for him the crowded croft,
   Nor the fertile flow of meadow;
   Not for him the sheltering shadow
Where the dew-damp soil is soft.

Monarch of deserted lands,
   Where no bee roams from the thicket,
   Lost to butterfly and cricket,
Robed in sober hues he stands.

HORSEMINT

Safe from scythe or ploughman's share,
   None molest and many love him;
   Even the ox that breathes above him
Browses by and leaves him there.

King is he o'er dearth and death:
   His dim colors have their glory,
   And some hint of far, faint story
Haunts the August of his breath,

Waking memories in my heart
   Of its childhood's Eldorado,
   Magic sunshine, shower, and shadow
In the land without a chart.

IN THE WOODS.

Deep in the woods I have loitered to-day;
Heard the hoarse bees droning summer away:
Saw the leaf-specters at games with the breeze,
And lured a gray squirrel to perch on my knees.

Plenty and peace were in love with the land,
Wild apples lifted their fruit to the hand;
Sweet was the nut and the mast of the pine,
But sweeter the gift of the wild grapevine.

I did not affect a rapture unknown
(May one not be honest when one is alone?)
But I left free my heart with Nature's to blend
And share all her secrets as friend shares with
    friend.

IN THE WOODS

But she, God's creation, is silent as God,
Dumb as the blossom she calls from the sod;
And her worshipper fancies 't is she that reveals
The wonders and signs that his own spirit feels.

Over the world from its far, quiet crest,
The sun-arrows shot aslant from the west,
And I know not what moved me from out of the
    years,
But that dying sunset was dim with their tears.

The forest grew darker, and sank to a hush,
Save the loud, sudden cry at the roost of the
    thrush,
And the audible silence, the breath of a sprite,
The wind and the delicate leaves in the night.

And in the weird spirit that autumn controls,
I thought I had felt the presence of souls,
The mystic desire of the heart ill at ease,
Which all men pursue and no man may appease.

TO SLEEP.

Wherein have I displeased thee, fickle Sleep,
   O, sweetheart, Sleep, that thou so far away
   Hast wandered and hast made so long thy stay?
I perish for some spell to call and keep
Thee near me, that thy gentle arts may steep
   My brain with calm, from dusk till dawn of day!
   The night's long hours are blind and love delay,
But, with thee, I would bless them that they creep.

Once, night by night, as love s own self wast thou;
   Over my boyhood's couch didst loose the powers
   Born of the opiate breath of autumn flowers,

TO SLEEP

And with thine own cool hand assuaged my
 brow;
Wherefore, I pray thee, keep not from me now,
 For I am summer, and thou art her showers.

www.ingramcontent.com/pod-product-compliance
Lightning Source LLC
Chambersburg PA
CBHW032222010526
44113CB00032B/289